WILD
OF THE

WILD FLOWERS
OF THE
PYRENEES

by

A. W. TAYLOR

1971
CHATTO & WINDUS
LONDON

Published by
Chatto & Windus Ltd
40/42 William IV Street
London W.C.2

*

Clarke, Irwin and Co. Ltd
Toronto

ISBN 0 7011 1807 5

Printed in Great Britain by
Bookprint International Limited

INTRODUCTION

Flowers of the Pyrenees present a picture which, though unique in beauty, is not as well known as it should be. The Pyrenees themselves, that great wall separating Spain from the rest of Europe, run for 240 miles eastwards from the Atlantic, to meet the Mediterranean at Cap Cerbère: they may lack some of the dramatic qualities, the extensive snowfields and the glaciers of the higher European Alps, but they possess a rich variety of mountain and valley scenery.

Two features, physical and climatic, which have important influences on the distribution and the nature of the plant life of these mountains must be mentioned here: the north, or French facing, side of the Pyrenees is steep, rising abruptly from the plain, and its river valleys are short; on the south, or Spanish side, the mountains fall away gradually over a wide area of sierras and hilly country, deeply cut up by long and wide river valleys. Furthermore, on the northern slopes, rainfall is heavier than on the southern, resulting in the heavily forested slopes of the French side, and contrasting with the arid sun-baked appearance of much of the Spanish slopes.

Again, there are wide differences between the western end of the mountain chain where, under the influence of the cool moist winds from the Atlantic, mist and cloud are frequent, and the Eastern Pyrenees where the higher temperatures, low rainfall and clear skies result in high sunshine records and low humidity.

This contrast between the Western and the Eastern Pyrenees is equally marked, with the influence of the Mediterranean becoming increasingly obvious, in the plant life as one travels eastwards: until in the Catalan Pyrenees of the far east, flowers of Mediterranean affinities become more and more frequent, even reaching considerable altitudes.

The traveller may be a little puzzled by some of the many beautiful flowers he will see in the Pyrenees. The smaller popular illustrated flower guides usually only deal with flowers of the Swiss Alps. The Pyrenean flora, though it shares many of the mountain plants and plant associations that are found in other European mountains, has been deeply modified by influences from Spain, and from the Mediterranean, while possessing a considerable number of species either peculiar to this range, or with more or less restricted distribution elsewhere, usually in the Southern Alps. It is hoped that this little book with its photographs of a selection of characteristic Pyrenean mountain flowers, both endemic and of more general distribution, all taken in their natural habitat, may be of some help to the visitor to these lovely mountains; and that it may persuade others to visit them. For nowhere else in Europe can be seen, in earliest Spring, wave after wave of daffodil species succeeding each other, colouring miles of mountain pastures and hillsides: nowhere else do the huge white spires of *Saxifraga longifolia* decorate vertical limestone cliffs, where the smallest crevices are studded with the rich purple of *Ramonda myconi*; nowhere else do the highest, barest mountain screes blaze with the golden suns of *Adonis pyrenaica*, or the highest mountain pastures scintillate with the piercing violet of *Gentiana pyrenaica*. All this, and much, much more, awaits the traveller.

Selection of the species illustrated has not been easy, but it is hoped that it maintains a balance between the endemic species and those of wider distribution: and also between the uncommon flowers, to be sought for in high places, and the common species which decorate every mountain pathside.

Finally, a word about the plates. The book is planned to show not only some of the Pyrenean wild flowers, but the mountains on which they grow, and the plates are arranged to give the most pleasing pictorial effect. The botanical classification can be seen in the Contents.

ABBREVIATIONS

cm.	=	centimetre (0·39 in.)
m.	=	metre (39·37 in.)
mm.	=	millimetre (0·04 in.)
sp.	=	species
ssp.	=	sub-species
var.	=	variety

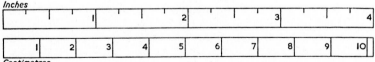

Inches

Centimetres

CONTENTS

Crocus vernus (Crocus purpureus) (Spring Crocus)

Family: *Iridaceae*

Leaves grasslike, usually appearing after the flowers. Flowers 5–7 cm. high, white, purple, or white veined with purple. In high mountain pastures up to 3000 m., flowering immediately behind the melting snow, and often accompanied by *Soldanella alpina*. *May–June*

Helleborus viridis (Green Hellebore)

Family: *Ranunculaceae*

Grows up to 20–50 cm. high. Basal leaves stalked, divided into 7–11 narrow-toothed segments. Flowers 2–4, large, of a pale green or yellowish-green.
Grows in open woods, alder scrub, and in open pastures up to 1800 m. *April–June.*

11

Prunus padus (Bird Cherry)

Family: *Rosaceae*

A frequent and beautiful tree in the Pyrenees, reaching a height of up to 15 m.; leaves oval and toothed, and the white flowers carried in drooping sprays in early Spring.

Grows in open woodland on mountain slopes up to 2500 m. *April–May*.

Erythronium denscanis (Dogstooth Violet)

For notes see next page.

Growing with *Ranunculus pyrenaeus*. Alt. 2600 m.

Erythronium denscanis (Dogstooth Violet)

Family: *Liliaceae*

Grows to 10–20 cm. high. The two opposite elliptic leaves are of a bluish-green, marbled with red. The solitary flowers are large and of a deep pink colour, with abruptly recurved perianth segments.

The species often grows in immense numbers in the high Pyrenean pastures, flowering immediately after the melting of the snow in Spring. Pastures and mountainsides from 1000–2500 m. *April–June.*

Narcissus pallidiflorus

Family: *Amaryllidaceae*

Leaves erect, flat and broad. Flowers drooping or horizontal, of a cream, or straw colour, sometimes bi-coloured with the trumpet of a deeper shade. Corona expanded and lobed at the margin, and the perianth segments imbricated and more or less twisted. This daffodil is one of the first of the early daffodils to flower in the high mountain pastures after the melting of the winter snows. Reaches an altitude of 2600 m. (Pyrenean endemic) *May–June.*

15

Ranunculus bupleuroides

Family: *Ranunculaceae*

A white mountain buttercup of the high Pyrenees. Resembling *R. pyrenaeus*, this plant has broader stalked leaves, and frequently carries more than one flower on the stem.

Grows in high mountain pastures to 3000 m. *May–July*.

Helleborus foetidus (Stinking Hellebore)

Family: *Ranunculaceae*

Leaves cut into 7–11 dark green narrow segments. The very numerous yellowish green flowers, cup-shaped and with a reddish margin, are carried in drooping and crowded clusters.
Grows in open scrub or on bare stony hillsides, often on limestone. To 1700 m. *February–June.*

Narcissus x bernardii

Family: *Amaryllidaceae*

Perianth segments vary from white to pale gold; central disc varies in length but is always short, and its colour varies from lemon yellow to deep orange. This uncommon Narcissus represents a natural hybrid between *N. poeticus* and *N. abscissus*. It is found in scattered colonies in high mountain pastures where both of its parents occur. Reaches 2600 m. *May–June.*

Fritillaria pyrenaica (Pyrenean Snakeshead) (with **Gentiana verna**)

Family: *Liliaceae*

Stem 20–50 cm. high, carrying one, or sometimes two, bell-shaped flowers of a dark purplish mahogany, chequered and marked with yellow. There is a wide colour variation. Leaves alternate, carried on upper two-thirds of the stem.

Flowers in early Spring in the high Pyrenean pastures, often in great numbers. *May–June.*

Astragalus frigidus (Phaca frigida)

Family: *Leguminosae*

A tall-growing hairless vetch, reaching a height of up to 45 cm.; leaves with 4–11 pairs of large oval bluish-green leaflets. Flowers pale yellow, fading to brown, in loose clusters.
In mountain meadows and in bushy places. To 1600 m. *May–July*.

Trollius europaeus (Globe Flower)

Family: *Ranunculaceae*

A tall, hairless perennial, 10–70 cm. high, carrying large globular yellow flowers, with overlapping and incurved petals on long stalks. A common and beautiful plant of wet mountain pastures and bogs. To 1600 m. *May–August*.

Ranunculus amplexicaulis (Pyrenean Buttercup)

Family: *Ranunculaceae*

Grows to 20–30 cm. high. Leaves oval to lance-shaped, bluish-green, and clasping the stem. Flowers 1–4, of a pure white, sometimes pink flushed, with golden centres.

Grows in Central and Eastern Pyrenees at altitudes of from 1500–3000 m. Often covers large areas of mountainsides; frequently accompanied by *Narcissus poeticus* and, in the damper areas, by *Caltha palustris*. Hybridises with *Ranunculus pyrenaeus*, giving rise to intermediate types. (Pyrenean endemic) *June–July.*

22

Vitaliana primuliflora (Douglasia vitaliana)

Family: *Primulaceae*

A prostrate plant, forming tufts or mats. Leaves in rosettes, linear-lanceolate in shape, and of a grey-green colour. Flowers stemless, axillary, of a bright gold colour, often so numerous as to hide the leaves completely. Grows in scree, and in the turf of steep high mountainsides, from 1800–2600 m. *May–July*.

Amelanchier ovalis (Snowy Mespilus)

Family: *Rosaceae*

A deciduous shrub 1–3 m. high, with small oval leaves white-woolly on lower surface. Flowers with 5 long narrow white petals, carried in clusters.
Often abundant on steep limestone cliffs and mountainsides. To 1400 m. *April–June.*

Pulsatilla alpina (Alpine Anemone)

ssp. alpina

Family: *Ranunculaceae*

Grows up to 20–35 cm. Leaves deeply dissected, of a light green. Stem leaves much smaller. Flowers large and cup-shaped, solitary. Flowers of *ssp. alpina* white, sometimes bluish on the reverse of petals. In *ssp. sulphurea*, flowers golden yellow.
Grows on rocky steep mountainsides, sometimes in open pinewoods, from 1200–2500 m. In the Pyrenees, in our experience, *ssp. alpina* is always found on acid formations, and *ssp. sulphurea* on lime. *May–June.*

Primula integrifolia

Family: *Primulaceae*

A small Primula, up to 5 cm. high, with almost unstalked bright green leaves, and flower stems carrying 1–3 large flowers of a clear rose-pink, the petals being notched.

Grows in damp, often shady places, where it may form mats. Usually on lime at altitudes of 2000–3000 m. *May–June.*

Scilla liliohyacinthus (Pyreneañ Squill) with **Narcissus abscissus**

Family: *Liliaceae*

From large bulbs, covered with yellow scales, spring wide glossy green leaves. The flower stems, up to 30 cm. high, carry loose spikes of pale blue flowers. Grows on open mountainsides, on stream banks, and among rocks, up to 2600 m. *April–June.*

Saxifraga exarata

Family: *Saxifragaceae*

Forms loose cushions of 3–5 lobed hairy leaves; flower stems 3–10
cm. high, carrying loose clusters of 3–8 cream-coloured flowers. A
frequent Saxifrage of cliffs and rocky outcrops. To 2800 m. *May–July*.

Ranunculus montanus (Mountain Buttercup)

Family: *Ranunculaceae*

A handsome large-flowered buttercup, 10–40 cm. tall. Leaves 3–5 lobed. Abundant in mountain pastures. To 1600 m. *May–August.*

Gentiana verna (Spring Gentian)

Family: *Gentianaceae*

This is the well known and much loved alpine Gentian whose brilliant blue flowers, springing from small rosettes of leaves, are to be seen on so many of the high mountains of Europe. There are many related species and forms, and the Pyrenean form illustrated is of a dwarf high alpine type growing in rock crevices at an altitude of 2400 m. *March–July.*

Narcissus abscissus

Family: *Amaryllidaceae*

Leaves erect, broad and flat. Flowers rather large, nearly horizontal. Perianth segments vary from pale yellow to deep orange yellow; corona deep golden yellow, narrow and straight, with abruptly truncated margin. The first of the early Daffodils over much of the Central and Eastern Pyrenees. A smaller and choice variety *Graciliflorus* occurs sparingly here and there.

Mountainsides and high pastures, also occurring on rocky outcrops and cliff ledges up to 2600 m. (Pyrenean endemic) *May–June.*

Pulsatilla vernalis (Spring Anemone)

Family: *Ranunculaceae*

This plant grows from 5–15 cm. high. Basal leaves dark green and deeply segmented. Stem leaves, stem, and flowers silky with long fine hairs. The large cup-shaped flowers are white within and pinkish without, above a collar of narrow stem leaves.

Grows on steep mountainsides and in high pastures from 1500–3000 m. Flowers very early in Spring, soon after the melting of the snows. *May–June.*

Iberis sempervirens (Evergreen Candytuft)

Family: *Cruciferae*

A low evergreen shrub, 10–20 cm. high. Leaves thick, oblong, and
dark green. Flowers white, in flattish clusters. Grows in screes and
on rocks from 1000–2500 m. *May–July.*

Narcissus poeticus (Pheasant's-Eye Narcissus or Poet's Narcissus)

Family: *Amaryllidaceae*

Leaves 7–8 mm. wide, of a bluish-green. Flowers carried on 30–50 cm. high stalks. Flowers white with central red edged disc. Intensely fragrant. Grows in immense numbers in meadows, on mountain-sides, and amongst rocks. Is found from quite low altitudes up to 2000 m. *June–July.*

Tulipa australis

Family: *Liliaceae*

15–30 cm. high. Leaves long and narrow, as long as the flower stems, which tend to be drooping. Flower buds streaked on the outer aspect with a reddish-brown, opening in full sun to show the brilliant golden interior.

Grows on rocky outcrops and rock ledges from 1500–2000 m. in the Eastern Pyrenees. *June–August.*

Astragalus monspessulanus

Family: *Leguminosae*

A tufted plant, 15–25 cm. high. Leaves long and narrow, cut into 20–30 oval leaflets. Flowers in loose heads of a pale lilac colour. Grows in dry stony places and on rocky slopes; prefers limestone. To 1500 m. *May–July.*

Geum pyrenaicum (Pyrenean Avens)

Family: *Rosaceae*

Grows up to 20 cm. high, with leaves showing a series of small leaflets with a large rounded terminal lobe. Flowers golden yellow, usually solitary. Grows on high alpine pastures, often accompanied by *Ranunculus pyrenaeus. May–July*.

Ranunculus pyrenaeus

Family: *Ranunculaceae*

10–20 cm. high, with 1–3 linear or lance-shaped leaves. Flowers white, usually single, but sometimes two on a stem.
Grows in high alpine pasturages from 1700–3000 m. May hybridise with *R. amplexicaulis. June–July.*

Rhododendron ferrugineum (Alpenrose)

Family: *Ericaceae*

An erect shrub growing to 120 cm. high. Leaves ovate, dark green above, rusty brown below. Flowers borne as terminal clusters, of a rich rose red.
Rocky places, steep mountainsides, and borders of woods, usually on acid formations, and growing to 3000 m. *June–August.*

Valeriana pyrenaica (Pyrenean Valerian)

Family: *Valerianaceae*

A stout tall-growing plant up to 150 cm. high; leaves dark green, broadly oval and toothed, with pointed tip; flowers pink, in dense terminal clusters.

Grows in moist or wet ground in woods and on river and stream banks, usually in deep shade. 1400 m. *May–July*.

Pedicularis foliosa (Leafy Lousewort)

Family: *Scrophulariaceae*

A tall-growing Lousewort, up to 60 cm. high, with long, finely-cut fern-like leaves. Flowers in dense clusters, of a pale yellow, with long leafy bracts.
Grows in wet mountain pastures and by streams, often on limestone. 1600 m. *May–July.*

41

Papaver suavolens

Family: *Papaveraceae*

The plant is bristly, growing to a height of 5–10 cm. The leaves are divided into irregular oval lobes, and are of a bluish-green colour. Flowers variable in colour but often of a delicate salmon pink. Grows at high altitudes of 1800–2500 m., usually in scree. (Pyrenean endemic) *June–July.*

Pulsatilla alpina (Alpine Anemone) (Yellow Alpine Anemone)

ssp. sulphurea

Family: *Ranunculaceae*

Grows up to 20–35 cm. high. Leaves deeply dissected, of a light green. Stem leaves smaller. Flowers large and cup-shaped, solitary. Flowers of *ssp. alpina* white, sometimes bluish on the reverse of petals. In *ssp. sulphurea*, flowers golden yellow.
Grows on rocky steep mountainsides, sometimes in open pinewoods, from 1200–2500 m. In the Pyrenees, in our experience, *ssp. alpina* is always found on acid formations, and *ssp. sulphurea* on lime. *May–July*.

43

Asarina procumbens

Family: *Scrophulariaceae*

A downy and sticky Pyrenean Snapdragon, with prostrate sprawling stems and opposite pairs of rounded leaves, shallowly lobed, and of a grey-green colour. The large solitary flowers are carried in the axils of the leaves, and are of a pale yellow, with a faint reddish marking. Grows in rock crevices, usually in partial shade, on cliffs and rocky outcrops. *May–August.*

Tetragonolobus maritimus (Winged Pea)

Family: *Leguminosae*

A low-growing plant with large light green leaves of three leaflets, with large stipules. Flowers solitary on 3–5 cm. long stems; colour sulphur yellow with keel of a darker yellow shade.
Grows in meadows, on damp hillsides, and on grassy banks, at altitudes of up to 1800 m. *May–July.*

Saxifraga aquatica (Water Saxifrage)

Family: *Saxifragaceae*

Grows in loose cushions. Leaves thick, dark green, semi-circular and deeply segmented. The thick flower stems, 25–60 cm. high, bear spikes of many white flowers.

Grows in streams and bogs at altitudes of 1500–2500 m. Usually accompanied by *Cardamine latifolia*. (Pyrenean endemic) *June–July*.

Antirrhinium majus (Snapdragon)

Family: *Scrophulariaceae*

A handsome perennial with narrow lance-shaped leaves and spikes of large reddish-purple flowers with yellow throats; height up to 80 cm. A yellow colour form is sometimes seen.
Grows on dry banks, stony places and roadsides. To 1500 m. *May–August*.

Lilium martagon (Martagon Lily)

Family: *Liliaceae*

A handsome and common Lily, with stems 1–1½ m. high, carrying
whorls of 4–10 lance-shaped leaves of a dark green, and clusters of
rather small pinkish-purple flowers with recurved perianth segments.
Grows in partial shade at the edges of woods and along fieldsides
and stream banks. To 2500 m. *June–July.*

Saxifraga longifolia (Pyrenean Saxifrage)

Family: *Saxifragaceae*

Forms solitary, large, long-lived rosettes, of narrow bluish green leaves, lime encrusted at edges. Flower stems 30–100 cm. long, bearing dense pyramidal spikes of many white flowers. The spikes are sometimes slightly drooping.

Grows in the crevices of sheer limestone cliffs, but sometimes also amongst boulders and on limestone debris. The plant dies after flowering. Is often accompanied by *Ramonda myconi* and *Campanula speciosa*. Occurs at altitudes of 1000–2200 m. (Pyrenean endemic). *June–July.*

Carduus carlinoides (Pyrenean Thistle)

Family: *Compositae*

This, perhaps the most handsome of all the thistles, grows up to 50 cm. in height, is white in colour, very spiny, with long narrow and much-divided leaves. The flowers, of a clear rose colour, are carried in clusters.

Grows on stony mountainsides and in screes up to 2500 m. *June–August*.

Anthericum liliago (St. Bernard's Lily)

Family: *Liliaceae*

Leaves basal and very narrow. Stems 20–40 cm. high carrying several small lilylike flowers. The whole plant and the flowers are smaller and more delicate than *Paradisea*.

Grows on stony, rocky hillsides and on rock outcrops from quite low altitudes up to 2000 m. *May–July*.

Coeloglossum viride (Frog Orchid)

Family: *Orchidaceae*

A small orchid, growing to a height of 6–25 cm. The greenish-coloured flowers are carried in a loose spike with prominent green bracts; the lip is three-lobed and tinged with reddish brown.
In high mountain meadows on limestone. To 1800 m. *May–July.*

Gentiana pyrenaica (Pyrenean Gentian)

Family: *Gentianaceae*

This remarkable Gentian, to be found at high altitudes in the Eastern Pyrenees, does not occur in the European Alps, but re-appears in the Carpathians. The stems, up to 6 cm. high, carry very narrow overlapping leaves, and the rich violet-coloured flowers are borne terminally. Grows in high, often boggy meadows, at altitudes of 1500–2500 m. *May–July*.

Arenaria tetraquetra

Family: *Caryophyllaceae*

A high alpine Sandwort, forming very dense hard cushions of tightly packed short stems which are covered by the overlapping round leaves: the white flowers, 4 or 5 petalled, are carried on very short stems.

This plant, found in the Central and Eastern mountains of the Pyrenees, grows in the crevices of rock faces and outcrops, in fullest sun. *June–July*.

Daphne cneorum (Garland Flower)

Family: *Thymelaeaceae*

A prostrate or dwarf shrub, sometimes reaching 30 cm. in height. Leaves narrow, blunt tipped, of a dark green. Flowers pink, very fragrant, in terminal clusters. A prostrate form, smaller in all its parts than the type, occurs at high altitudes in the Eastern Pyrenees, and is sometimes known as *var. pygmea.*

Grows in turf and on rocky outcrops, both on limestone and non-calcareous rock, at altitudes of up to 2500 m. *May–July.*

Androsace vandellii (A. imbricata)

Family: *Primulaceae*

One of the high alpine cushion-forming members of the genus. The tufts of small overlapping silvery leaves are compressed into a domed rounded cushion which, in flowering time, is often entirely covered with the stalkless white flowers, yellow throated, and honey scented. Grows in partially shaded or overhung crevices of granitic cliffs from 2000–3000 m. *June–July*.

Linaria pyrenaica (Pyrenean Toadflax)

Family: *Scrophulariaceae*

A tufted perennial, of blue-green colour, reaching a height of up to 20 cm. The leaves are narrow and undivided, and the tightly packed heads of long-spurred large lemon yellow flowers have orange in the throat.

Grows in scree and rock crevices at 500–2000 m. *May–August.*

Antirrhinum molle (Soft Snapdragon)

Family: *Scrophulariaceae*

A delicate plant, trailing, or semi-erect in habit. Stems 10–25 cm.
bearing small soft oval leaves, very woolly. Flowers white, or pale
yellow, marked with gold in the throat, and borne in the axils of the
leaves.

Grows in crevices of rock faces, preferring a semi-shaded site.
Occurs on the southern side of the Pyrenees. Altitude up to 1600 m.
(Pyrenean endemic) *June–July*.

Aquilegia pyrenaica (Pyrenean Columbine)

Family: *Ranunculaceae*

Grows to 20–40 cm. high. Leaves three-segmented and deeply divided. Flowers large, and of a clear pale blue; spur slender and slightly curved.

Grows in steep, partly shaded meadows and mountainsides, at edges of woods, and amongst boulders, from 1500–2500 m. (Pyrenean endemic) *June–August.*

Anthyllis montana (Mountain Kidney Vetch)

Family: *Leguminosae*

Stem woody at the base, 10–30 cm. high, with leaves bearing 8–20 oval leaflets. Whole plant very silky. Flowers rose coloured, in crowded heads. Grows on rocky outcrops at from 1500–2000 m., usually on limestone. *June–July.*

Geranium phaeum (Dusky Cranesbill)

Family: *Geraniaceae*

Leaves deeply cut into 5–7 lobes; flowers carried on 30–60 cm. high stems in long-stemmed pairs; colour a dusky purple, and of a characteristic flattened form. A frequent and attractive flower of shady river banks and at the edges of woods and pastures. To 2400 m. *May–July.*

Lonicera pyrenaica (Pyrenean Honeysuckle)

Family: *Caprifoliaceae*

Forms bushes up to 120 cm. high. Leaves small, rather narrow and pointed, of a bluish-green colour. Flowers cream coloured, fragrant, and borne in pairs.

Grows in crevices of cliffs, and on steep, rocky slopes. Found on limestone up to 2000 m. (Pyrenean endemic) *June–July*.

Lilium pyrenaicum (Yellow Turkscap Lily)

Family: *Liliaceae*

A handsome lily, 50–100 cm. high, with leaves dark green, narrow, and closely packed on the stems. The flowers, yellow with dark spots, may number up to 12 on a stem. In gardens the flowers have a rather unpleasant scent, but in the wild this does not appear to be so. Grows amongst boulders, on cliffs and steep mountainsides, and rarely in meadows. Altitude 1000–2500 m. Pyrenean endemic *June–July*.

Genistella sagittalis (Chamaespartium sagittale)

Family: *Leguminosae*

A small shrub with creeping, woody stems and erect almost leafless stems 10–30 cm. high, with conspicuous wide green wings. The golden-yellow flowers are carried in dense terminal clusters.

On stony hillsides and in dry pastures, usually on limestone. To 1600 m. *June–August.*

Himantoglossum hircinum (Lizard Orchid)

Family: *Orchidaceae*

One of the larger and perhaps the most striking of European orchids. Grows to a height of 30–70 cm., with pale green leaves and long spikes of up to 80 flowers. These are composed of a rounded greenish helmet with an extremely long lip divided into three very narrow greenish-grey lobes.

Grows on roadsides, dry banks, and in meadows. Frequent in some parts of the Pyrenean foothills. Up to an altitude of about 800 m. *May–July.*

Rosa pendulina (Alpine Rose)

Family: *Rosaceae*

Forms bushes from 30 cm.–2 m. high. Stems upright, often without prickles. Leaves bright green, of 7–11 leaflets. Flowers bright pink to cerise.

Grows on mountainsides, in open woodland, and in stony places, up to 2500 m. *June–July.*

Cytisus purgans (Sarothamnus purgans) (Pyrenean Broom)

Family: *Leguminosae*

A small bluish-green shrub 30–60 cm. high. Leaves undivided and
alternate; flowers golden yellow in terminal clusters, scented.
Widely distributed in the Eastern Pyrenees, particularly on the
Spanish side; grows on steep stony mountainsides up to an altitude
of 2500 m. *May–July.*

Saponaria ocymoides (Rock Soapwort)

Family: *Caryophyllaceae*

Grows in loose clumps, composed of many branches bearing small oblong hairy leaves, dark green in colour. The bright pink flowers, with short stalks, are borne in great profusion.

Grows in dry stony places and on rock faces. Prefers limestone: may reach 1500 m. *April–August.*

Polygonum bistorta (Bistort)

Family: *Polygonaceae*

Perhaps the most beautiful member of the Dock family, this species reaches a height of up to 100 cm. The lower leaves are egg-shaped with winged stalks, and the pale or bright pink flowers are carried in dense terminal spikes on unbranched stems.

A characteristic plant of mountain meadows. To 2400 m. *May–August*.

Silene acaulis (Moss Campion)

Family: *Caryophyllaceae*

Forms mats or domed cushions of small narrow pointed leaves, of a bright green colour. The flowers, carried on very short stems, are of a bright pink which varies in depth of colour.

Grows in rock crevices, on scree, and sometimes in short turf. Found on calcareous and non-calcareous formations, from 1900–3300 m. *June–August.*

Paradisea liliastrum (St. Bruno's Lily)

Family: *Liliaceae*

Leaves basal and narrow. 3–5 pure white, large, lilylike flowers carried on stems 20–50 cm. high.
Grows in alpine meadows, and on mountain-sides from 1000–2500 m.
June–July.

Campanula patula (Spreading Bellflower)

Family: *Campanulaceae*

A slender biennial growing to a height of 60 cm. Leaves narrow lance-shaped, and the large blue-violet flowers with spreading petals are carried singly in wide clusters.
Grows in sub-alpine meadows. To 1700 m. *May–August.*

Anthyllis vulneraria. var. coccinea (Red Kidney Vetch)

Family: *Leguminosae*

A common and handsome mountain Kidney Vetch; leaves with up to five pairs of leaflets, hairy on lower stems. The bright red flowers are carried in rounded heads, and the calices are white-woolly.
Grows in stony places and dry meadows, often on limestone. To 2500 m.
May–August.

Gentiana alpina (Southern Gentian)

Family: *Gentianaceae*

Leaves in small tight rosettes, of a yellowish-green colour, and almost as broad as long. Flowers almost stemless, bell-shaped, of a clear deep blue, white in the throat with blue spots. This Gentian does not flower as freely in nature as others of its group.

A high-growing Gentian occurring at altitudes of 2000–3000 m. Grows in high mountain turf, and on rocky outcrops. *June–August.*

Adonis pyrenaica (Pyrenean Pheasant-Eye)

Family: *Ranunculaceae*

Grows to 30–40 cm. high. Leaves bright green, deeply cut into thin segments. Flowers 4–6 cm. in diameter, of a bright golden yellow. Grows in steep scree, and on rocky outcrops from 2000–3000 m. altitude, in the Eastern Pyrenees. Very local. (Pyrenean endemic) *June–July.*

Linum alpinum (Alpine Flax)

Family: *Linaceae*

A perennial plant, 10–30 cm. high, with lance-shaped leaves of a bluish-green, and clusters of large bright blue flowers.
In meadows and stony places, usually on limestone. To 1600 m. *May–July.*

Ranunculus thora

Family: *Ranunculaceae*

The slender stems of this mountain Buttercup carry 1–2 small golden-yellow flowers, but the striking feature of the plant are the very large rounded leaves of a grey-green colour, solitary and clasping the stem.

Grows on stony mountainsides and in clearings in woods. A high alpine form is found on the highest mountain screes, where it reaches a height of only 5 cm. or less. Usually on limestone. To 2800 m. *May–July.*

Campanula speciosa (Pyrenean Bellflower)

Family: *Campanulaceae*

A stout plant, 30–50 cm. high. Leaves in basal rosettes of long narrow wavy-edged leaves, very hairy. The very large handsome blue to violet flowers, bell-shaped, are tightly packed on the thick fleshy stems.

Grows on limestone cliffs and scree, up to 1800 m.; often accompanied by *Saxifraga longifolia* and *Ramonda myconi*. (Pyrenean endemic) *June–July.*

Ramonda myconi (R. pyrenaica)

Family: *Gesneriaceae*

Grows in flat rosettes of dark green crinkled leaves, hairy above and woolly below. Flowers 1–6 on stems up to 10 cm. long; colour of a pale to deep violet, with golden centres.

Grows in shady crevices on sheer cliffs, often of red sandstone or limestone.

May be found growing on isolated boulders and may occur in woods. Found throughout the Pyrenees up to 2000 m. though usually at rather lower altitudes. Often accompanied by *Saxifraga longifolia*. (Pyrenean endemic) *May-June.*

Vicia onobrychioides

Family: *Leguminosae*

A straggling Vetch, 50–100 cm. high. Leaves with 12–16 pairs of narrow leaflets. The flowers, of an intense blue-violet colour, are carried on long stems in loose one-sided clusters.

Grows on stony hillsides, on rocky outcrops, and by roadsides. Often on limestone. *May–July*.

Potentilla rupestris (Rock Cinquefoil)

Family: *Rosaceae*

Grows to 40 cm. high. Plant much branched, leaves downy with
3–7 leaflets. Flowers white, in loose clusters.
Grows on rocky slopes up to 2000 m. *May–July*.

Dianthus carthusianorum (Carthusian Pink)

Family: *Caryophyllaceae*

Grows from 10–50 cm. high. Leaves narrow and pointed. Flowers borne on long stiff stalks, in heads of 2–10; colour of flowers varies from a bright pink to a deep red. Below the flowers are stiff brownish bracts.
Found in stony, hot situations, usually on limestone. Reaches 2000 m.
June–August.

Asphodelus albus var. pyrenaeus (Asphodelus sphaerocarpus) (Pyrenean Asphodel)

Family: *Liliaceae*

Leaves, long, narrow and stiff, forming large clumps. Flowers white
with brown bracts, in large spikes on stems 100–150 cm. high, usually
single, but sometimes branched.
Grows on rocky slopes and mountainsides from 900–2000 m.
(Pyrenean endemic) *June–August*.

Globularia nudicaulis var. gracilis

Family: *Globulariaceae*

A tufted herbaceous plant up to 10 cm. high; from the basal spoon-shaped leaves arise leafless stems carrying rounded heads of pale blue flowers.
Grows in meadows and stony places. To 2800 m. *May–July.*

Reseda glauca

Family: *Resedaceae*

Forms compact clumps of narrow bluish leaves with the whitish flowers carried on slender 10–30 cm. long stems.
In rocky places and screes, usually on limestone. To 2600 m.
June–August.

Gentiana lutea (Great Yellow Gentian)

Family: *Gentianaceae*

A stout plant $\frac{1}{2}$–2 m. high. Leaves large, elliptical, bluish-green in colour. Flowers golden yellow with brown spots, carried in clusters terminally, and in upper leaf axils. In alpine pastures and stony hillsides up to 2500 m. *July–August.*

Aconitum vulparia (Wolfsbane)

Family: *Ranunculaceae*

Grows to a height of 50–150 cm. Leaves dark green and 5–7 lobed, each lobe being further divided. Flowers yellow, in elongated helmet form, carried on tall stems.
Stream sides and amongst boulders up to 2500 m. *August–September.*

Phyteuma halleri (Dark Rampion)

Family: *Campanulaceae*

The tallest of the Rampions, growing up to 60–90 cm. high. Leaves toothed, heart-shaped at the base, with stem leaves narrow. Flowers in compact heads, dark violet in colour with prominent bracts. Grows in damp meadows from 1500–2000 m. *June–August.*

Rhinanthus alectorolophus (Great Yellow-Rattle)

Family: *Scrophulariaceae*

A semi-parasitic plant, a very common and colourful component of sub-alpine and alpine meadows. The pale green leaves are long and toothed, and the flowers are carried in terminal spikes, yellow in colour, and interspersed with leafy bracts.
Abundant in mountain meadows. To 1500 m. *May–August.*

Galeopsis pyrenaica (Pyrenean Hempnettle)

Family: *Labiatae*

Grows to 10–30 cm. high. Leaves oval, slightly toothed at edges.
Flowers borne terminally and in axils of the leaves; flowers pink,
fading to pale purple, with the corolla longer than the calyx.
Grows on high steep screes, usually on basic rock, at altitudes of
2000–3000 m. (Pyrenean endemic) *August–September.*

Meconopsis cambrica (Welsh Poppy)

Family: *Papaveraceae*

A perennial plant growing from 30–50 cm. high. Leaves light green and deeply divided. Flowers yellow, sometimes streaked with red, on stalks arising in the axils of the upper leaves.
Found in diverse habitats, from the semi-shade of river banks to steep high mountain scree. May reach 3000 m. *July–September.*

Centaurea montana (Mountain Cornflower)

Family: *Compositae*

A stout perennial plant, reaching 10–80 cm. in height; leaves narrow lance-shaped, of a bluish-green colour. Flower heads large, solitary and of a dark blue colour. A plant of mountain meadows and stream-sides. To 1600 m. *May–July.*

Viola cornuta (Horned Pansy)

Family: *Violaceae*

Leaves ovate to heart-shaped. Flowers on 20–30 cm. stems, blue-violet, with a long spur.
Grows in high meadows and in alpine pastures to a height of 2500 m.
Often associated with *Narcissus poeticus. May–August.*

Sempervivum arachnoideum (Cobweb Houseleek)

Family: *Crassulaceae*

A plant forming mats of silver rosettes, the silvery appearance being due to the densely hairy tips of the leaves. Flower stems 4–12 cm. high, bearing heads of deep rose coloured flowers.
Grows on rocks, cliffs, and screes, reaching a height of 3000 m. *June–August.*

Rhaponticum cynaroides (Cardoon Knapweed)

Family: *Compositae*

A very handsome giant Knapweed of the Pyrenees. Reaching a height of up to 1½ m., this plant has very large, deeply cut leaves, dark green and hairy above, white-downy below. The stems, often unbranched, carry large rose-purple flowers 6–7 cm. across, with many narrow brownish bracts. An uncommon plant, growing in high, steep and rocky places up to 2500 m. *July–September*.

Juniperus communis. ssp. nana (Dwarf Juniper)

Family: *Cupressaceae*

A dense, spreading shrub, with whitish-green needle-like leaves; the globular fruits change from green to bluish-black.
Grows in rocky and stony places, often covering boulders with its mat-like growth. To 3000 m. *June–July.*

Pinus mugo var. rostrata (P. uncinata)

Family: *Pinaceae*

A common Pine of the Pyrenees, reaching a height of up to 25 m., with greyish-brown bark and dark green leaves. Grows in rocky places up to 2200 m. *May–June*.

Merendera pyrenaica

Family: *Liliaceae*

A bulbous plant, allied to Colchicum, flowers almost stemless, composed of six strap-shaped segments not forming a tube at their base; rose pink in colour, with occasional albino forms. Flowers appear in early September before the leaves, which are usually produced in the Spring.

Occurs in the high Pyrenean pastures from 1500–2500 m., often in very great numbers. (Pyrenean endemic) *September–October.*

Crocus nudiflorus

Family: *Iridaceae*

The common autumn-flowering Crocus of the Pyrenees. The large
rich purple flowers appear in September, and may be found until the
coming of the first snows. As the name implies, the flowers appear
before the leaves, which are not produced until the following Spring.
This Crocus is peculiar in its method of increase by underground
stolons.

Occurs from near sea-level to 2000 m., and may be seen in vast
numbers in the high Pyrenean pasturages. *September–October.*

Euphorbia helioscopia (Sun Spurge)

Family: *Euphorbiaceae*

A handsome Spurge growing to a height of 10–40 cm.; the leaves are oval and smooth, and the broad flat-topped heads of flowers are of a golden yellow colour.
Grows in mountain pastures and on hillsides. 1800 m. *May–August.*

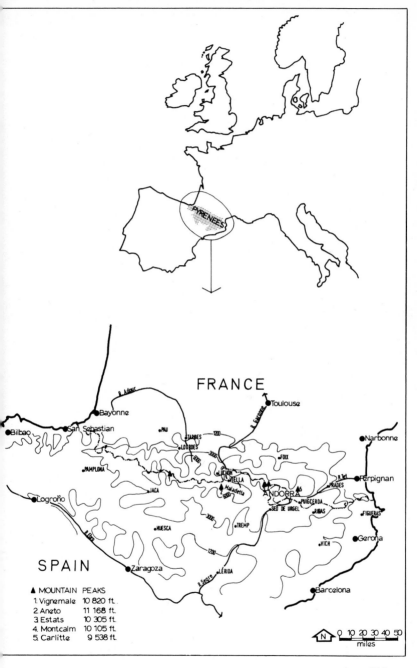

FRANCE

● Bayonne

R. Adour

Toulouse ●

R. Garonne

● Bilbao

● San Sebastian

● PAU

● TARBES

● LOURDES

1200

3000

● FOIX

● Narbonne

● PAMPLONA

LUCHON

● VIELLA

Maladetta

2

1

ANDORRA

5

● SEO DE URGEL

PUIGCERDA

● PRADES

R. Tet

● Perpignan

● Logroño

● JACA

3000

RIBAS

● FIGUERAS

● HUESCA

● TREMP

3000

● VICH

● Gerona

SPAIN

1200

● Zaragoza

R. Ebro

R. Segre

● LÉRIDA

● Barcelona

▲ MOUNTAIN PEAKS
1. Vignemale   10 820 ft.
2. Aneto   11 168 ft.
3. Estats   10 305 ft.
4. Montcalm   10 105 ft.
5. Carlitte   9 538 ft.

N   0 10 20 30 40 50
          miles

INDEX